GETTING PLAYED

The ultimate guide to a
healthy relationship

MOHOSHO POFANE

Kindle Direct Publishing

*To my best friend, lover, companion, partner,
and soulmate (you know who you are)*

"I am nothing special; just a common man with common thoughts, and I've led a common life. There are no monuments dedicated to me and my name will soon be forgotten. But in one respect I have succeeded as gloriously as anyone who's ever lived: I've loved another with all my heart and soul; and to me, this has always been enough."

NICHOLAS SPARKS

CONTENTS

INTRODUCTION

Bob Marley once said "the biggest coward is a man who awakens a woman's love with no intention of marrying her." But what about a woman who awakens a man's love with no intention of marrying him? Well, that's a topic for another book!

Love is a beautiful thing. It's a risk that most of us take over and over again with the hope of finding the perfect partner with whom we're willing to spend the rest of our lives. Someone who will make the love journey worthwhile. While we're searching, we end up in toxic situations, being played or ghosted, as a result end up looking at the whole notion of love differently. Some people give in to the cruelty and play the game too, while others keep hoping for a good partner on try over and over again. It's often said that the world does not reward those who play by the rules (which is arguably true), so wouldn't it be great if we knew the difference between people who come to us to play and those who come with genuinely good intentions?
We all know the feeling of being played in dating. You were misled by someone who seemed to be into you.

There were no warning signs that someone was about to flip the script but just as you were letting your guard down and starting to get excited about the promise of a long term relationship, the person you were dating totally flakes. They pull away. They dump you. They ghost.

At the end of the day leaving you feeling like a fool for believing in something that clearly was not real. So how can we avoid getting played or made to feel like a fool in dating? First understand what it means when someone plays you. Essentially they have tricked you into giving up something that you would normally never give up unless you were guaranteed to get something in turn. This could be sexy time, money, time, or intimacy. But a player makes you believe in the promise of a return on your investment. They make you feel like you can trust them, when in fact they are completely untrustworthy.

This book does not expose anyone as you'd think. It makes no reference to anyone and it is based purely on observations and research. Thing is, most girls secretly wish they had a male best friend. One who would tell them all about boys, their conversations, their daily plans about women, everything. However, those are rare to find because under normal circumstances, your male best friend is only hanging around because he's patiently hoping that one day you'll give in and he'll hit it. That's if the two of you haven't made that 'mistake' already. It's through our friends of opposite sex that we get the kind of information contained in this book., although most content in this book is more oriented to the females. Either way, take this book is your companion who is not patiently waitng to sleep with you.

Since some chapters talk about general dating, everyone can gunner up something from this text, male or female. After all, it is the ultimate guide to a healthy relationship.
Personally, I've had my fair share of playing women, and I have friends who still master the game, single and married. This is not something to be proud of honestly but sometimes circumstances can lead you there. For example, I personally lost faith in dating some time between end of high school grad and university. At that time because my ex-girlfriend from high school had cheated on me and consequently ended our relationship. That was when I left my small hometown to begin my new journey at university. I had invested so much in that relationship it started to feel like all women are the same: cruel, ungrateful and cold as I found her to be (we're still good friends though).
Since then I never committed to any relationship. I learned anything and everything that I thought would help me score as many women as I could. The body count was the only thing I could think of. There is something that parents and teachers always told us that "stay away from relationships and focus on your studies, you'll get as many women as you want at university". I find that statement to be entirely true. In case you're wondering, I've been with all kinds of women I had a little fetish in, from skin colour, social

status,body size, height you name them. While at it, I've had my heart broken, caught feelings, got hit on, got involved in petty fights and before I forget, I ended up in hospital at this time. But that's a story for another book too.

Fortunately, people outgrow these bad habits and behaviour and learn from their mistakes, sometimes they learn the hard way like I did. The most important thing is that hurting one's feelings is wrong notwithstanding the amount of reasoning you attach to your little games. It is wrong and unnecessary. I cannot even go on about the negative effects in your life that come with it. You just cannot go around using and hurting people just because someone from your past that they don't even know did the same thing to you years ago. Some time later you might get tired of all these games and finally decide to get married to the love of your life, you'd want to have kids and live happily ever after. But what then if you get cheated on left right and centre?
All I'm saying is, we need to start treating others like we'd want them to treat us. We need to have compassion and respect for the feelings of others. When I wrote this book, I thought of all the people who are going to fall victims to someone who behaves the way my friends and I did long ago. I thought to myself, "what if it's my own daughter?", what if it's my nephew or someone I love?" Then I decided that since I may not be there to guide them or give them a little pep talk about men, I might as well write a book, something they can keep referring to every time things get out of control.

I'm not saying the book will completely help, but it's always good to know the truth, the decision is always yours!

PREFACE

It's in rare cases that one can just wake up and write a book based on wisdom and experience alone. When it comes to relationships, one does not stop learning. Relationships surprise even the most qualified professionals in human psychology. Even so, in 2015 during the peak of my dating game at Law school, I felt like I've heard enough. I had already got my heart broken multiple times and had broken many too. Eventhough I knew there were new challenges ahead, something told me that with the little wisdom I had, I should put it on paper, then improve it over time, esspecially for my nephew who had just been brought to earth then. My heart sank to the thought of how she's going to fall a victim to some of the things she could've avoided should she have been warned. So I began writing this book, the warning. It was an incredible journey, especially when some of my ex partners would think some extracts were about them, especially the sidechick topic. Anyway wisdom is wisdom, it does not matter how or from whom it was acquired. This book is about how to not get played in dating.

CHAPTER II

HOW PLAYERS CAN BE IDENTIFIED

Here Are Some Common Characteristics Of Players You May Need To Know:

- Although they come in all shapes and sizes, players are usually above average looking.
- Any man who has 5 or more girls crushing on him is by default transformed into a player.
- Unlike the common guy, they don't flirt. Or they do it rather subtly.
- If you meet them online, the first chat would probably turn into a sexy time chat.
- They'll ask you for nude pictures.
- They'll want sexy time. They won't be very explicit about the commitment part.
- If you say no to any of the above, they'll leave you
- You won't see them after the one night stand
- They'll only have anything to do with you if they want to sleep with you again.

- Although age is no bar, they are mostly guys in their late teens and 20s.
- They love to ask for money or favours.

Read The Signals

Most often than not, it's not that difficult to tell if one is a player or not. They usually lay it out there but because they're really smooth at what they do, you'd probably be too infatuated to read the signals. The common words that players usually say are "Please don't fall for me" and "I'm not good for you". They usually say this after they had taken you out on a date or after sleeping with you – proving themselves as ideal boyfriends and more.

They put extra effort in what they do and it's easy for girls to mistake this for love. Remember I said that anything a player does for you is in fact intended to impress the next girl. So the road trips and fancy getaways aren't only for you but for all the potentials that you are likely to tell how much of a gentleman he is.

This rubs off even the slightest possibility of finding the truth about him because your new experience with him will be the total opposite of what his victims claim. They're just bitter that I've found love, you'd think. While in actual fact they're just looking out for you.

Players have a habit of telling you exactly who they are, and for some magical reason this usually works for them. How many times have you found yourself in a situation where a guy says to you "But I told you not to fall for me?" realising that even after he'd on countless times tried to hint you that you shouldn't fall hard, you did anyway.

The other useful hint is that players will often tell you the kind of women they prefer, they're not afraid to tell you this even on the first date. If he tells you he prefers slim women, immediately do yourself a favour and do a quick introspection of yourself. If you're not what he says he prefers, there's a high likelihood that he's going to leave you when he scores himself a preferred prey. They may say this jokingly or in passing, either way, run!

Ask Yourself The Following Questions:

Do I Feel Weakened By His Looks?

The truth is some men are good looking. I know here you're probably wondering if I'm straight but the truth is the truth. Some of them are just too smooth with words and incredibly irresistible. They can get you wet from just saying "Hi" and by the time they ask for your number your mind would be almost close to climax. I hate to tell you that the minute this happens to you you're in trouble.

Intuition will slap you so hard and by the time you wake up the next day he'll be so gone. The only thing in your possession will be a blouse that smells like him, constantly reminding you of how trashy men are. Therefore, it is important to always make sure that you are in control of the situation and nothing about a man affects your rational thinking.

Does He Seem More Intelligent Than You Are?

You're most likely to subject yourself to someone who seems a little smarter than you are. This usually happens subconsciously. If that is the case, the odds are high that you may agree to anything he says if he seems a little bit smatter than you are. Players usually notice when you envy them and they use that to their advantage by ordering you around - even if it means making you think less of yourself in order for them to be in control.

In such situations, your confidence is very important because if it fails you, he is going to make you seek the validation you need from him and it never ends well. I always preach that self-confidence, self-love and self-respect are not sexually transmitted and one cannot get them from dating or sleeping with players. Instead, you'll get the opposite!

What Is He Known For?

As typical as that sounds, doing a little background check is a very crucial consideration before considering a relationship. You don't want to find yourself with someone who openly embraces cheating for example, or one who is known for bringing home a new girl every week. The idea here is to not get blinded by his fame and fortune or any other material object he possesses.

Do you ever wonder why a rapper would call women hoes and all other degrading words and still manage to take them home after the gig? Yeah... it puzzles me too.

Anyway there are typical examples of a fame that 'may' not be good for you, you just have to evaluate if that fame is intended to impress women or it comes out of pure hard work or talent.

That is to say, players do everything and anything to stand out from the rest of the crowd even though some girls are merely impressed by their incredible body count, perhaps it's out of curiosity - they want to know what it is about these men that so many women cannot have enough of.

The Hunters And The Hunted: Don't Be The Easy Prey

The girls who aspire such dashing, swashbuckling men only always without a fail know the reputation of these guys or at least know how popular they are among other girls. It is important to establish how many other girls have a crush on them.

Players know that girls always behave in a herd mentality in the sense that what other girls approve of is always golden and they must have it at any cost. This way they start ignoring all the red flags and just don't mind testing the waters for themselves in the hope that they will get lucky and the guy will magically transform into a no-fault Prince Charming one day.

Ladies must understand that they cannot change men;

a man will only change if he wants to change and not because someone wants him to. If you decide to date a player, the end result is always the same; you get played.

The girls who are overconfident of their physical charms always disregard what wise old people always advised: power corrupts and absolute power corrupts absolutely. So in a nutshell, some girls claiming to be the victims of these players usually know well beforehand the risks involved in dating them. It's sour grapes only when they realise their utility is over and the players won't ever trade their freedom for a baseless commitment.

That is when the name calling of all men is bred, with the general assumption that all men are as messed up as the previous guy. It is important to note that players are basically narcissistic people who always place their self-interests and pleasure over everybody else's. Because they got plenty of choice before them, they make full use of it.

You're probably wondering if players ever reflect on their actions, the answer is no, they hardly ever regret anything. Like a fisherman planning on his next fishing adventure, players only think about how they will smash the next girl before end of the month.

The caveat emptor rule applies everywhere in life and relationships are no exception. You only have yourself to blame if you're going to offer physical intimacy (inarguably the most cherished jewel a girl possesses and should trade cautiously) on a platter at the blink of an eye to a guy you know very little about - who has not declared or proved his long-term commitment to you. However, it would be unfair to lash out only at players because it always takes two to tango ... so why should they harbour any feelings of guilt when all guys secretly wish to be like them and all girls swoon over them because they are no ordinary mortals?

My dad used to tell me it's an unfair jungle out there and survival of the fittest is the name of the game. Naturally there would be only two types of animals, the hunters and the hunted – so, "Ghoda Ghas se yaari karega to Khayega kya?" loosely translated: a stud and sweet, juicy grass can't ever be friends.

CHAPTER III

*WEAKNESSES THAT RENDER US
SUSCEPTIBLE TO GETTING PLAYED
IN DATING:*

They'll Play If You Can't Say "No."

L earning to say "No" is the first step in never getting played because No is the most powerful statement in dating. No is what we are all afraid of hearing and it is the reason why we put ourselves through so much drama. No is a denial, it's a rejection. No says, I'm putting my needs first.
The ability to say no to someone and not feel guilty, or "like a bad person," is one of the most powerful gifts you can give yourself.
If you want to avoid being played, you have to learn how to say no without coming across as childish. Your no has to be in power and not in protest. You can't spring a no on someone that you're dating after having

said yes a million times. It would appear to be a red flag. After all, usually when your partner suddenly disagrees to something that they always agree to, there is a high likelihood that he/she may be cheating, lost interest or just doesn't feel like doing it in all honesty.

It's only at the minute you start to miss the person you're dating that you will go back to saying yes to any-thing they want.

You'll Be Played If You're Afraid To Lose Your Partner

We get played in dating because we are afraid that if we don't give in, we will lose our partner's person's inter-est. Never be afraid to let someone walk away. Our fears vary as to why we risk a part of ourselves for the affec-tion of someone else.

Maybe we fear that we will never feel this good again. Maybe our chemistry has been altered and now we've bonded with this person in a way that we've never bonded with someone else. Maybe this person triggers our ego and we need to prove our worth through their affection.

Whatever the reason, you have to remember that los-ing the wrong person is never a bad thing. You have to notice when you're acting out of anxiety and fear of loss.

If someone is threatening to walk away because you aren't giving them what they want, it is apparent that you are being used, and you are in a prime position to be played. Often times we're willing to feel bad apart from someone we care about just so we can justify being with them. If we only feel good when we're with them, we rationalize, then it must be real.

However, think about this. If you only feel good when you're with someone else, you're actually perpetuating a fantasy. The truth is, what you have to offer will be accepted by the right person and rejected by the wrong person.

You'll Be Played If You Don't Create Boundaries

There's a saying: any plan is better than no plan and some boundaries are better than none. Boundaries are a very confusing concept to most, especially when it comes to creating boundaries in dating. Boundaries are the safety zones where you feel good.

When someone oversteps a boundary you have created, you know it because it makes you feel bad. Setting any boundaries is better than no boundaries at all in dating. If you decide that you won't spend money on a first date, or that you don't go out with someone you met on social media before speaking on the phone then those are your boundaries.

Author Tony Robbins interchanges boundaries and rules by asking the following questions: What are the rules for dating you? What can someone do and not do? What is allowed and what isn't allowed? By establishing your own rules or boundaries, you make it harder for someone to push past them.

It's when we don't set boundaries or worse, when we ignore them that we make ourselves vulnerable to predators. If you don't kiss on the first date, then you shouldn't change that behavior because someone else thinks you should. Stick to your rules, and those who don't want to play by them can go ahead and kick rocks.

You'll Be Played If You Don't Ask More Questions

It's easy for us to be played when we are afraid to ask questions. It might sound insecure or boringly interrogative to want to know more details but the truth will set you free.

For example, if the person who'd asked you out cancels a date, don't be afraid to ask when you can plan another one, although that alone can stand as a red flag. Your date must prioritize the date you've set for yourselves, if not it should be cancelled on time, at least two days before the date, not two hours before the date or a day before. Some people prepare for a date psychologically and physically. So you can't cancel a date after they'd bought a new dress, went to a spa treatment or cancelled a night out with friends, it's just rude.

However, if the person you're dating doesn't return your text, don't be afraid to ask them if they received it. If the person you're dating is behaving in a way that is bringing questions to your mind, then don't ask your best friend, ask them directly before you get paranoid.

Our unwillingness to ask questions is really our inability to handle the answers. The truth might reveal that this person isn't that into you. The reality is, they aren't. They are playing you and you are going along for the ride.

Imagine yourself being promised to be taken to a destination. The day then comes and you hear nothing from your date, three days later you get a shady explanation that could've been made a long time ago. Players make promises that they have no intention of keeping. When they divert from the original route, that's why you should ask questions to why. If you're not asking questions to hold your date accountable then you're going to get played.

You'll Be Played If You Allow Bad Habits

If you do anything once, it's an accident, if you do it twice it's a pattern. If you do it three times then it becomes a habit and habits are hard to break.

When the person you're dating asks you to make concessions, you have to assume that this behavior will continue the duration of your relationship. If you don't want to be the person always going out of their way then don't start the trend. For example, if your date wants you to go out of your way to see them and you don't want to continue to be the one going out of your way, just say no. Ask to reschedule the date when it's more convenient for both of you.

Getting played is about giving today on the hopes that you will be given something better later. Unfortunately, there is no way to know that you're investing in the right person until you actually know them. Before you give someone more than you're comfortable with such as your body, your money or your time, you should ask for what you want sooner than later.

For example, you spend a lot of money on your date. The next time you want to make plans you ask them to split the bill and they refuse. You shouldn't hedge your bet and think that in the future things are going to be different. If you don't want to get stuck paying for all dates, plan a date that's free or just leave the whole thing. To expect that they will reciprocate before you have actually asked them to is dating on potential. Sure they could, but will they?

If you are making assumptions that when you're ready to recoup on your investment the other person will gladly reciprocate then you're dating on potential not the reality. If you don't want to get stuck in a behavior that you don't like, don't agree to it in the first place. If the other person dislikes your boundaries then they aren't for you. It's that simple.

CHAPTER IV

*HOW TO PLAY A PLAYER INTO A
SERIOUS RELATIONSHIP*

Playing Hard To Get

What will work for you in this case is if you play a little hard to get. If you were wondering whether it's possible to make a player fall in love with you, there you have the answer! Although you have to consider that hard to get will only pan out when interest has already been detected, even if it is a slight interest. It has been established that:

- People who play hard to get are more likely to land a date or relationship over those who make it too easy.
- Individuals who appear "interested" during the date and committed in conversation are often perceived as appealing, but also considered easy conquests.

- Individuals who come across as disinterested, however, seem fascinating to suitors because they appear more difficult to get, and they peak curiosity.
- When you make it a bit harder for a suitor to get your attention, you are perceived as having greater value as a partner, and the challenge is a turn-on to your date.
- Playing hard to get also increases attraction. The more they think about you the better the chances of them falling in actual love.
- Playing hard to get makes women seem cautious when picking a partner. It prevents us from simply settling for anyone.
- Women increase the possibility of starting a relationship by upholding their standards.
- That sexy sense of mystery a man creates when playing hard to get makes women more intrigued and vice versa.
- It results in meeting a "long-term" partner and establishing a committed relationship.
- If you're a woman who's not looking for a relationship, but rather casual sexy time, there is no benefit to playing hard to get.
- When someone does not appear to be so available, the more likely a potential partner will want to spend time and money on them.

However, There Are Some Important Considerations To Bear In Mind...

1. Cat-and-mouse play is all fun and games until someone gets hurt.
2. Whenever there are emotions involved, you risk the chance of someone being more invested than the other.
3. If you are planning on walking the walk and talking the talk with playing hard to get, do it with class.
4. It should be fun for both sides and it's never (in any situation) attractive to be stuck up.
5. Even if you are the one playing hard to get, you may fall... hard.
6. Go into the game knowing it may not turn out the way you planned.
7. Play wisely, play fair and have fun!

Are You Over Your Last Hurtful Relationship? Here's How To Handle Your Next:

After being single for a while, or after being in a relationship that hurt you badly, you've opened yourself up to love again. You think you might be in love with your boyfriend, but you're looking for signs of true love before you say those three magical words.

If you've been hurt before (and I'm going to bet you have), it may be hard for you to make yourself vulnerable enough to let this man know you have serious feelings for him. It's worth exploring those feelings a bit first to ensure what you're feeling is really and truly love.

Either way, no matter how deeply in love you feel like you are with a man never be the first one who says the following deal breakers, or else you'll be signing up for being played like never before:

- I think I'm in love with you
- You mean the world to me
- I can't imagine life without you

My mother always told me that the first mistake we make as people is to put humans before God. That is to say, if a human being means a world to you or you cant live without one, then what is God to you? She mentioned that the reason why people lose themselves after breakups (resorting to alcohol, cutting friends etc) and even commit suicides is because they'd invested their all in a person and people, unlike God are unrealiable. If your partner disappoints you, there's absolutely nothing you can do about that but does God ever do?

Now that I've shared my mother's wisdom with you, allow me to tell you that sometimes a man might just not be ready for a serious relationship or hasn't figured out yet if he has feelings of true love for you. And saying the above might just turn him off, chase him away or he may choose to take advantage and play you.

I mean, let's be serious for a minute, how were you able to live all this time before you met your partner? Men are wired to hunt and they are hunters in nature. They find no pleasure in taking home a dead moose they found across the road. But for a deer that they spend the entire day hunting, they will most likely show it around to their friends and hang it's head on the dining wall as a trophy so that everyone can see it.

The Difference Between Love, Lust, And Infatuation

Is it love or infatuation? Sometimes it's hard to tell but one thing men know about women is that for them, attraction overrides intuition.

You may think that your days of being infatuated with a male were long gone after high school, but intelligent women of every age go through being infatuated. It is part of the journey to love, but it's easy to mistake infatuation for love.

When you're infatuated, you have an overwhelming attachment to a guy. You can't get enough of him. The problem is, as researchers discovered, infatuation causes a lot of negative emotions like anxiety, insecurity, and nervousness. You haven't yet been with this man long enough to be certain of his feelings, and so every little thing can send you in a tizzy of worry.

For example, if:

He hasn't texted you back in 49 minutes! He must be out with another woman! You'd think.

He made a weird face during sexy time. Did he not enjoy himself? You'd think.

Therefore, infatuation is often more based on the idea or fantasy of a person than the reality. You may build him up to be something better than he is simply because that's what you want. Infatuation is a temporary state, so if this feeling starts to fade, you know that it's not love.

Lust, on the other hand, is more based on physical attraction. You can feel lust for someone that you have no emotional or intellectual connection with (that's pretty much the definition of the hookup). If you're always eager to jump in bed with this guy, but really don't get that much out of spending time with him otherwise, you're likely in lust, not love.

But love sweet love is total and consuming...and it lasts. It may take longer to blossom as you open yourself up to a man and get to know him in return. But with love, you can be yourself, and you recognize that neither of you is perfect.

So which one are you feeling? It may be hard to know (though lust is a pretty easy feeling to identify). Take your time to process your feelings. As you get to know him better, you may feel differently toward him. And over time, you'll likely see some of the signs of true love I discuss up next.

The Importance Of Going On A First Date

It's easy to realize that the problems in most relationships and families are simply rooted in the fact that partners never took some time to know each other before engaging in anything. Some were force by circumstances to spend time together or to get into marriage and later begin to realise that they have married the wrong person. I cannot stress enough how necessary and important it is for people who intend to get into relationships to embrace the culture of having first dates.

Dating is basically going through an exponential growth phase. It is fun, exciting even, to go on a date with a person who is practically a stranger. That is because first dates give people the ability to create a new persona for themselves in order to come across as the person they want to be, rather than the person they actually are.
Everyone is on his or her best behaviour on first dates. They become very cautious of every move they make and they become the person they think will impress the most.

They do this by sitting up straight and eating small bites of their lunch while employing their best manners. They present themselves as an improved version of who they really are. The likelihood is that they will go along with the majority of what the other person has to say in order to avoid conflict even when in reality they completely disagree.

If you look back on your first date with an ex or current, you'll probably remember them to be very different to who they are now. They probably don't do things they used to insist on doing on your first date because the relationship has reached a more comfortable stage like paying the bill or driving. (That was just to impress you) And this isn't such a bad thing. It can be a sign of comfort with one another, taking the relationship to the next level and an element of mutual respect and equality.

Everyone knows that first dates are a make it or break it kind of thing. They set the bar for how the rest of the relationship is going to play out. You're either going to get a good impression of the person and think 'oh okay he's cool or I'd be up for seeing him again' or cut things as short as possible, ghost him, and avoid him at all costs.

One bad date can put you off dating forever. But how are you going to learn about what you like and what you don't like in the other person than through experimentation? Don't consider first dates as 'putting yourself out there' and doing something you're not used to and comfortable with.
Consider them as qualitative market research for the study which is you. Think of it as primary data collection in a subjective manner. Getting out into the field (Dinner, lunch date etc.) is the only way you're going to figure out what you're looking for in a partner. After you've done your research, you can analyse the results, and reach your conclusion.
This will make things clearer for you and when you have a more clear idea of what you want, you can simply go out and get it.

CHAPTER V

*THIS IS WHAT BEING IN LOVE
TASTES LIKE, IF YOU CAN'T RELATE,
YOU'RE GETTING PLAYED*

How Many Of These Signs Of True Love Ring True For You?

Even if you've been in long term relationships in the past, you may not be certain you ever really experienced true love. You may have been in your early 20s when you met the man you ended up marrying; however, at that age could you really have understood love? Love changes over time, and what it looked like for you as a young adult is likely quite different from what it looks like today.

If you're experiencing several of these signs of true love, you can feel good, knowing that, at long last, you finally found it!

Your Partner Makes You Want To Be A Better Person

Oprah talks about being your best self, and while much of that work has to come from within, being with the right person can make you want to be even better. One of the signs of true love is recognizing that neither of you have to be perfect, but you can inspire one another to be better.

Think of the couples who exercise together or eat healthier. Now think of couples where one person exercises or diets while the other keeps on with the same bad habits. Which relationship do you think is more love-based? Right! It is the one where the couples are partners in better living.

Maybe your partner has made you more aware of the need to recycle. Or walk to work. Or simply be nicer. Whatever that thing is, you feel better by starting new healthy habits.

You Want To Be There For Them In Good Times And Bad

When you date someone that you just like, you might be uncomfortable when sh#^ hits the fan. Maybe his parent dies or he's worried about being laid off. What's your role if the relationship isn't serious?

On the other hand, when you're in love with someone, you are happy to be there for him when things get tough. You're willing and able to be strong for him, to let him lean on you as he deals with stressful or traumatic situations. You know he'd do the same for you.

You're Confident In Your Relationship

Like I said before, when you're infatuated, you can be insecure and nervous in a relationship. Every little thing feels like it's rocking the boat, and you worry you'll be tossed overboard (break up). But one of the signs of true love is having confidence in your relationship. You know that every argument won't be the end of your relationship. You don't worry that he's out flirting with other women. You know your relationship is strong enough to weather a few bumps, and you're willing to put in the work to make it better.
You don't sweat the small stuff, and you know that you are enough for this man.

You Can Be Yourself Completely Around Him

It's completely normal to want to shine the best light on yourself possible when you first start dating, but as the relationship progresses — and as your feelings get stronger — you should be able to relax a little and be more genuine. That means you're okay with him seeing you without makeup or in your ancient fuzzy pjs. One of the signs of true love is simply knowing that no matter what you say or do, you won't run him off, nor are you afraid of what he'll think.

Maybe you snort when you laugh. Let it out.

Maybe you fart in your sleep. Again, let it out!

Maybe you talk really fast and ramble. He can handle it.

Realize that, as he's falling for you, he's doing the same thing. He might be paranoid about his big stomach, so he's been sucking it in. Or maybe he snores. But as he relaxes around you, he sees that he doesn't have to worry about you judging him for these things. Because when you're in love, none of those little things matter.

You Allow Yourself To Be Vulnerable

When you're truly in love, you are willing to expose your heart to potential pain. Love is trusting that this person will not break your heart.

If you find yourself still closed off after a traumatic relationship, you might not quite be exhibiting one of these signs of true love, but give it time. It can take a significant amount of time — even years sometimes — to get over serious heartbreak and be open to falling madly in love again.

So what does vulnerability look like? When you say what you really want and feel, you open the channels of communication, and you make room for actually getting what you want. You can let him know that, because you've been hurt in the past, you're finding it hard to be open now. But don't rush it. If being vulnerable doesn't come naturally, you may need to work through some past experiences that are blocking you from falling in love again.

You're Done Playing Games

Games are most definitely for children, though I'm willing to bet your younger self played a few when dating. Still, another of the signs of true love is that you have no desire to play with this man's mind. You want to be straightforward so that he knows you're serious about where this relationship is headed.

So let's say you're having an argument with your boyfriend. Game Playing You would have stormed out, hoping he'd chase after you and beg for your forgiveness. But the Real You knows that this is no way to be in a relationship, and so you express your frustration and seek a way to resolve the situation.

Congrats! You're a mature woman in a relationship...in love!

You Want To Do Nice Things For Him

You give to him because you love him, not to get something in return.

You're at a bookstore and you see a book that your boyfriend would love, so you buy it for him. You don't do this so he can reimburse you for the book, or so you can rack up "points" with him. You don't even care about him returning the favor. You simply want to do something nice, without reward or thanks.

This is, to me, one of the best signs of true love, because you are acting from a completely selfless place. You are putting someone else before your own needs and desires, and that is truly a beautiful thing.

It Is Not Fleeting

Like I said earlier, infatuation is fleeting. You may feel crazy in love for a few weeks early in a relationship, but after a while, his habit of chewing with his mouth open makes you so angry that you think about breaking up for this insignificant reason. This isn't love.
Love goes on and on and only grows over time. The more you get to know him, the more reasons you have to love him. Often with infatuation, the more "real" things you know about a man, the less you like him. But love is the opposite. You don't gloss over the negative, but you take it as part and parcel of being with this person long-term.

One Argument Does Not End The Relationship

I remember the first few arguments I had with my girlfriend when we first started dating. I remember worrying that each would be the end of our relationship. But as I started falling in love with her, I remembered that those arguments were less scary. I was more confident in my love for her, and knew that a silly disagreement wouldn't end us.

You See Him In Your Future

Everything you think about in the future — from a camping trip you have planned in six months to living abroad in 20 years has him in it. One of the signs of true love is simply seeing a future together and talking about it. You're not just fantasizing about walking down the aisle to marry him; you can picture the small stuff too. You can see taking ski vacations at Afriski. Selling your house when the kids move out and moving into a small condo by the beach in Cape Town.

It Feels Natural

Loving him just feels right!
Love should never ever feel forced. I know women who wanted so desperately to be in love that they tried to maneuver a not-right relationship into love.
It never worked out.
If you're really in love, it just feels... right. You don't worry about the whatifs and shoulds because you know they'll just magically work themselves out. This man fits with you, with your life. When it's right, there's nothing more natural than love.

You Would Gladly Sacrifice For Him

The two of you have been invited to a party at your friend's house... but his friend from college is in town the same night. Rather than fighting about it or trying to guilt him into going to the party, you tell him you'll hang with him and his friend.
Or you move in together and you pick a flat that's a shorter commute to his job... and twice as long for you. You don't begrudge him for getting his way because you

love him. And you know that he'd sacrifice for you just as much. Love makes not having your way not feel like a sacrifice; you're simply doing it in the name of love.

His Successes Are Yours

He got a promotion at work and you're thrilled. Same goes for when he just has a great day. You're looking at one of the signs of true love when you're genuinely happy when he does well at life.

You're supportive of him as he works his way through law school or anything else that's tedious and time-consuming. When you love someone, you are there for him emotionally through the ups and downs, and you show that you're cheering him on. It's a huge confidence-builder to know someone cares about you enough to be his own private cheerleader!

It's Not All Roses And Unicorns (And That's Okay!)

When you were younger and fancied yourself in love, you foolishly thought every minute would be magical. You felt sad and confused when things were less than perfect.

But now you realize that loving someone means there is good and bad. Your relationship might be great for months or years, and then you hit a rough patch. That doesn't mean things are over; it's just part of the cycle. At this point in your life, you understand that there's no such thing as perfect when you're in a relationship. But there is happiness, and that should be your aim.

You're Truly Partners In Life

Maybe when you were married or in a long relationship, you didn't really feel like your mate was your equal partner. Maybe one of you dominated the relationship, throwing everything off kilter. But with this guy, you really get the sense of equality.

You take turns being the strong one for the other person when you're going through something tough. You both work hard to make your relationship solid. You each give and take in a balanced way. You don't have to keep score because you know he's putting in just as much love as you are.

You Don't Rely On Him To Make You Happy (Though He Does)

A common problem I've seen in my experience in dating is when one person turns to the other to feel happy. Then things go badly when that person doesn't pay enough attention to the other, or if she spends time with friends instead of her man.

I know you've probably heard this before, but let me say it again: you can't rely on other people to make yourself happy.remember I said that we shouldn't put humans before God, that way we won't feel a need to end our lives when all turns sour.

Here's a concept for you to mull over: experts say that your relationship with another person mirrors the relationship you have with yourself.

Sit with that for a minute.

If you can't make yourself happy, you can't expect someone else to. On the other hand, if you have a good relationship with yourself, love yourself and are happy on your own, you'll have a good relationship with your partner. You'll know that, while he makes you happy, that's not his job. And you'll know that you can 100% be happy on your own.

You Communicate, Not Fight

Communicate with love rather than fighting.

It's completely normal to have disagreements when you're in a relationship. But it's how you deal with those that determines how strong your relationship is. Between a couple that shouts at one another and calls each other names… and one that sits down and gets to the root of the issue… which one do you think is likely to last longer?

Another of the signs of true love is being willing to communicate rather than fight. You might be effing furious at some perceived offense, but rather than blowing up at him (because what does that solve?), you take a walk around the block, collect your thoughts, then come back to discuss the problem rationally. This actually produces positive results. He finds out what he did wrong and can make the situation better, and he doesn't feel defensive when you talk to him.

You Love To Make Him Smile

Ahh, one of my favorite things in the world is to make my girlfriend smile. It's like a gift! If you're in love, you will be eager to make your mate smile. You can do that with small or big gestures: an unexpected kiss, a love note stuck in his lunch, or a six-pack of his favorite beer chilled in the fridge can be enough to make him feel warm fuzzies.

You Would Do Anything For Him

If someone had told you a year ago that you would be...
...watching football and liking it...
...eating something you used to think was disgusting...
...or playing board games with his nieces and nephews on a Saturday night...
...you wouldn't have believed them. But being in love makes you willing to compromise, to do things you never thought you'd be willing to do. And it's okay because he does the same for you: maybe you talked him into getting a manicure or getting his teeth cleaned up at the dentist during the holidays. Being in love puts you out of your comfort zone, but more often than not, you end up realizing you love something unexpected!

People Say You're Perfect Together

So maybe you're still unsure whether you're seeing signs of true love yourself... so look to what your friends are saying about you as a couple. Maybe they're constantly rolling their eyes at how darn cute you are.

Or maybe friends who knew you when you were in your previous long term relationship say you seem so much happier with this guy than you were for decades.

You have one perspective of your relationship, and your friends have another. Try to see yourself how they see you.

You Can Accept His Flaws

You don't mind his beer belly because you love him.

You never thought you'd end up with a guy with back hair (just like Charlotte was with Harry on Sex in the City), but it turns out he's pretty perfect for you.

Or maybe your man has a lisp… and you kinda find it adorable.

We all have flaws, but love has this way of turning them into assets. If you find the fact that he sings (terribly) in the shower endearing, you, my dear, just might be in love!

You Want To Live Together/Have Kids/Get Married

When you got into that terrible break up, you may have sworn up and down that you would never love a man again or even live with a man. But this guy has you thinking differently. Maybe you thought you'll never have kids until you are at least in your mid 20's, but now you yearn to have a Mini Him running around.

Especially if you've been through a challenging relationship in the past, being able to envision a future with a new man is a huge step! Congratulations.

He's the First Person You Turn to with News

Okay, here's a scenario to imagine: you just got a huge raise at work or you've just been told you won a competition. Who's the first person you call?
If it's your boyfriend, that's a good sign of true love. When you love someone, you want to share news (good and bad) with them.

You're Always Excited To See Him

It could have been a day or week since you've seen your boyfriend; doesn't matter. You're just as happy to see him. You never get tired of being with him, and when you're apart, you have so much to catch up on, even if nothing really happened in his absence.

You Spend Time Apart...But Think Of Him

I've said this before: strong couples spend time doing things separately. You love spending time together, but you also have your monthly book club, happy hour with the girls, and your gym time. You miss him, of course, but you feel better for having some 'You' time.

You'd Rather Watch Movies On The Couch Than Go Out

When you first started dating, you liked being wined

and dined, checking out the hot new restaurants in town. But now that things have settled down, you're even happier just having a Netflix and Chill night on the couch. You don't need to be impressed with fancy dinners; popcorn and beer are an excellent accompaniment to his company.

You've Told Him Everything About You

When you're in love, you're not afraid to tell him all your deep, dark secrets. You have nothing to hide because he will accept every part of you. Opening up like this is hugely vulnerable, but it's a great step in your relationship.

So all in all, I'm betting that you've nodded your head while reading these signs of true love and now realize that, heck yeah, you're in love! The question is… does he feel the same?

Don't let the way you feel colour the way you interpret how he feels for you. Pay attention to how he acts around you: does he seem to feel the same, or does he push you away sometimes?

You'll fall in love at different tempos, so don't be heartbroken if he's not there yet. The important thing is that you now have identified your feelings as true love! Let the rest come in time.

CHAPTER VI

IT'S NOT ALL THE TIME THAT A PLAYER PLAYS – YOU CAN PLAY YOURSELF TOO

Here's How:

The truth of the matter is that not every man who cannot hold a long term relationship with you is a player. Apart from all the other selfish self-serving reasons, there could be some personal reasons as to why he left and they find it hard to communicate them. The most common of those reasons are:

How Your Feminist Views Can Chase Your Partner Away

Some feminists have a subconscious (and probably conscious one as well) hatred towards men... they see men as oppressors, abusers and rapists.

Social media posts that highlight these issues often linger on in their minds and create extreme reactions that surface when they experience problems in a relationship. Initially you are tagged as "A different or an exception to the list', slowly they come to a conclusion that 'you too are a man hence no different."

Relationships with feminists can become hard to deal with and probably one that bring only pain but you and your partner can close both eyes and mouth on gender equality, fair attitude towards men and return affirming comments on radical feminism and even proclaim like all those feminists that feminism is equality, then your relationship may last a while. Women must understand that if a few men are abusive; there are over a million who give up their lives fighting in a war or working as corporate slaves to feed their wives and children and make them smile.

Bad Hygiene Is Always Intolerable

I always find it odd that couples would engage in many sexual activities without a problem and only be covered in shame when they have to talk about hygiene. Hygiene is the one thing that couples should be openly discussing because it affects the relationship drastically.

However, it still remains very difficult for couples to talk about hygiene in relationships and as such, I've gathered opinions and comments from different people with different experiences so that you can individually deduce what keeping good hygiene really means to your partner.

> My girlfriend has really bad hygiene. We live together and sometimes her lady parts smell so bad to the point where I barely can stand being in the same room.

> I went on a date and this guy smelled so bad I legit threw up... why do I even try?

> So I liked this really hot guy, smelled nice all the time... I thought he was the cleanest person ever until I got the chance to see his undies which had skid marks. I was so confused.

> I had a date and I thought he was nice. I'm not seeing him again though because he had bad teeth. He looked like he never brushed his teeth. I couldn't ever kiss him.

So I hooked up with this chick a few days ago. She is pretty awesome but she smelled bad down there. Big turn off.

I made out with a man who was drunk and had bad breath. Now, I can't kiss anyone who has slightly bad breath or else the memory of him and that night comes back.

I never told my ex that he had bad breath. He hurt me bad, but I felt like that would be an immature attack.

I broke up with my boyfriend once I saw the size of his member and how bad it smelled.

My girlfriend has really bad hygiene. We live together and sometimes her lady parts smell so bad it's to the point where I barely can stand being in the same room

The comments above don't necessarily mean one cannot score a serious relationship because of them. They're supposed to give us a general view of how our habits or bad hygiene can affect others while we are unaware of it. It means we should try harder or be cautious of such details since it appears rather difficult to discuss them as partners.

Some of the complaints raised above cannot be rectified. That is because some people have serious health problems that need medical attention or that everything they've tried didn't help. It is in this case that we really have to be supportive of our partners and discuss ways to get them help without offending them.

Some other small yet major causes of ghosting are discussed further below:

They Just Didn't Enjoy The Sexy Time.

Sometimes 'it's not you, it's me' is just a cry out for bad sexy time experience. Your date would rather choose to break up with you or completely disappear than to expressly tell you that the sexy time was terrible – even women do this. Most women hold a position that all sexy time is the same but believe me it is not.

The best we can all do is to look after ourselves. It it very difficult to go back to a person who gave you a bad sexy time experience, let alone explaining why you cannot see them anymore. Although sexy time isn't supposed to be the sole decider for a long term relationship, a lot of people seem to base their decisions on it.

One Bad Kiss Could Also Cost You A Relationship

I personally find it childish that people choose to run away from a bad kisser when they can simply teach them how to do it. Learning how to kiss is such a small yet romantic adventure for anyone to run away from. Unfortunately there are people who take it so seriously that they would completely disappear if the first experience goes terrible. Therefore it's important that you pay attention to kissing and avoid being a bad kisser in case it costs you a potentially good relationship

It's easier with women because they're usually able to help each other out and teach each other some of this romantic adventures. However, men find it rather hard or completely inappropriate to kiss another man meaning their options are only limited to females. It's never a dull moment to simply ask your partner to teach you how to kiss properly.

CHAPTER VII

GENERAL DATING

How Respect Affects Your Relationship

A view from 'The Feminine Woman'
Elderly people used to tell us that women aren't looking for respect. Women are looking to be protected and led by someone who has a backbone. They want a leader and they want to be loved and cherished by that strong, principled leader.

We're told that back in the old days women respected their men because they feared them to some degree... men had the power to break their necks in less than 15 seconds. Today this fear is virtually gone, as feminism and political correctness has chipped in and made us all question the essence of maleness, along with the sexual tension/polarity that comes from the masculine/feminine dynamic

We could argue that men work tirelessly the whole day forgetting about the things they want in life, they hardly buy themselves anything just to bring something home and some of these men never even get a thank you from their spouses. Their spouses rather accuse them of not making enough, while consecutively comparing their hustles. They belittle and bruise their manhood egos, let alone those who struggle for jobs every day, running up and down in the sun looking for piece jobs, sometimes even going extra to do things that haunt them forever. These men be feeling like losers, feeling depressed to go home to a woman who will insult them, who sometimes don't even prepare them a meal, robbing them off their manhood.

Everybody knows men crave respect in an intimate relationship with a woman. However, it's not always automatic to give it. Lately I've been toying with the idea that respecting a man is not 100% always a woman's conscious choice, specifically in an intimate relationship situation.
Let's hear the details below from a conversation I had with Anon so that we can draw our own conclusions about the notion of respect in relationships.

Anon: I feel deep respect for my fiancée, and it's not logical. I don't tell myself to respect him. He earned it by not being willing to be a passive man. I feel respect. It's in my gut, it's in my heart, and it exists as a part of my body. This respect feels like a part of me, almost like the lifeblood that runs through my body.

However, I have also chosen to give respect to him even when I was scared.

Do you feel the same? Do you think that respecting a man is not your choice? Perhaps it is something you have to feel for a man?

Men Who Command A Woman's Respect Automatically

Anon also said that she believes there are some men in the world, a smaller population of men, who command respect from a high-value woman automatically.

"You walk past them in the street and it's just the way he carries himself, the way he walks past you without checking you out and instead is fully focused on his mission in life; and he is true to that mission 100% and knows his place in the world – you can't help but respect him."

But we could also argue that a woman who holds herself as low value might just chase after him and try to sleep with him and hope he will marry her, while indeed a high value woman will silently acknowledge him under her breath and give him respect instinctively.

I agree a lot of men don't deserve the respect from women; they talk a lot and do little, like many women do anyway.

Nevertheless, when it comes to a relationship with a man, here's what I suggest:

You may not respect him fully yet but give him the

benefit of the doubt for at least one month. You have to give yourself a chance to feel respect for him and give him a chance to be the man, unless of course he is useless as a man in a relationship. I admit that some men just like to walk through life getting easy sexy time and not caring about anyone but their mom.

That's if they even care about their mom. They like to just check women out and seem to have no idea that human beings have feelings; and that women have souls, deeper than just being a piece of meat. These men are probably not worth your time.

You don't have to respect any man who is not worthy of your respect outside of dating or a relationship but when it comes to dating and having a relationship with a man, respecting a man matters, for the health of the relationship between you both.

If you don't start off respecting a man in any way at all, it bruises his manhood, and the foundation of your connection falls to pieces. He can't be the man you want him to be in the relationship, after all, you don't even believe in him. You're not giving him that gift. And if you don't believe in him, he won't trust you, or commit to you fully. He's going to doubt you and feel insecure.

On the other hand, if you start off dating a man coming primarily from fear – you can't show respect or feel respect anyway. You're not even there yet, because you are too fearful, and too much in survival mode.

Another thing...

The majority of women in this world prefer to marry up - to heighten their social status, to be more financially stable... to be with a man who is more intelligent and makes more money than her. It's instinctive. It doesn't mean they can't marry a man who makes less money than they do – provided you respect him and are really attracted to him, it doesn't matter.

Biologically, women are driven to seek men of status; and to seek men of higher status than they are.
Men know women seek high status men and here's why that matters in relation to respect:
Men know intuitively, that women prefer to seek men of high status. They know that intuitively. They can't always say that, but they do know it. Meaning if you are criticizing him, and if you are pointing out everything you think is a flaw, and if you can't let him take you places and make decisions, he will automatically feel emasculated, and he won't commit fully to you.

He might be casual with you, but he won't commit fully to you and eventually leave or ghost you. After all, there's no reason to. He doesn't get one of the most crucial things he wants from a woman; which is respect.
If you don't respect a man – your eyes show it, your body language shows it, the words that come out of your mouth show it. So he feels it. And if he feels that you don't trust him; that's a sign to him that you don't see him as a valuable, respectable man.

Be Honest With Yourself About The Type Of Man You Really Want

Although I am almost certain that respecting a man mostly isn't your choice (though I'd like your input on this one), I do believe that in the beginning stages of a relationship, you are both quite unsure and don't know each other that well yet; so you need to give him the benefit of the doubt. And when you do this; many men will step up to the plate and be that strong, powerful man for you; earning your respect, but in any long term relationship, you can't just call him weak or emasculate him and expect him to be the man you want him to be.

This is why it's crucial for you to not just go for any man who seems willing and available to have a relationship with you.

Not only are you hurting yourself, you're hurting him.

If you want an alpha male, if you want a high status man, don't pretend that you don't. Be honest with yourself; be authentic. Don't cheap out and go for a man you're not really attracted to because you feel desperate for a relationship. A lot have done this before and it's essentially a complete fraud. Provided you're too scared to go for a higher value man; and I guess for good reason: that you've not become a high value woman yourself yet.

Is Respecting A Man Really Your Choice?

I still believe that if you are choosing to date a man; that you need to at least have the courage to respect him first for at least one month, unconditionally. But don't expect respect in return unless you are a high value woman either or unless you genuinely choose to be there dating him.

It has become obvious to me that many people throw the word respect around as if they own it. You'd hear them say: "I don't respect that person, I have no respect for them; they did this, and they did that; oh what a loser." – Well, the truth is, nobody respects you either.

Don't claim you don't respect people just so you can feel all high and mighty for a minute. People can feel that empty clawing for a moment of significance and self-importance because you feel like you are small. Genuine respect is felt. Genuinely give respect where it is due, and if you are unsure whether to give respect; give them the benefit of the doubt.

We cannot ignore the fact that there are also many people out there who prefer to sit on the couch and do nothing their entire life and who have no respect for anyone. Well, they don't even respect their own existence in this world; they don't even respect the life they've been given.

If you are able to give a man that you've chosen to date respect to start with, then, over time, you will see, and learn more about him. And you can make your decision from there.

Here's Where You Can Start With Men. How To Give A Man Respect:

In most relationships that I observe today, it's the woman who wears the pants and the man remains passive. In reality, he's scared as hell. His balls are in her jar, up in her secret little hiding cupboard.

Unless you are a naturally masculine woman, this isn't

your natural place. It's not your place to emasculate a man and not trust him to do anything, or make any big decisions, or feel the need to point out what they should do and where he went wrong.

So try not wearing the pants for some time with the men you meet.

Don't be passive either; that doesn't work. I know that most women who hear this will go and be passive instead; and start operating from another extreme.

But – don't sit there waiting for a man to do everything; you can give a suggestion, but trust him enough to let him make his own decisions for you both about where to go, and YES – let him make every mistake under the sun in his life without telling him what to do.

The reason you don't want to do this is the reason you have to do it. Because it scares you.

That's what it means to be with a man; allowing him the opportunity to be a man for you, and to make his own mistakes. He will want to do better for you when he sees that you will accept him even when he stuffs everything up. That's the way men test women.

Even if you feel you are too scared to do this; try anyway. You can always leave the relationship if you want. You won't die from it.

So with all this 'Talk' about respect, respect, respect, you might wonder; what is respect, and what it means to respect a man. Here are some suggestions on how to respect a man.

How To Respect A Man:

(Choose from these options based on whether you're just dating for a short while or looking for a long term relationship. I trust you to choose.)

And if you are more masculine that's fine. Ignore these because you may not want a relationship where the man is masculine and you are feminine. Choose another type of relationship that is true to you.

*Respecting a man means to not wear the pants (literally).

*To give him the gift of your joy and not withholding your joy out of fear.

*To respect the fact that he has an ego and this ego needs to feel good. You have the choice to laugh at that and say to this: 'what a joke' – that's up to you. But it all depends on how much you genuinely want a relationship and want true love and not just a significance trip for yourself. People can feel the difference between these two, by the way.

*When he makes a mistake, don't say: "I told you so." or "Remember when I told you not to do that?!" Find something more compassionate to say. He's a human being.

*Smile and enjoy the fun when he forgets a turn off or goes in the complete wrong direction. Oh. No? Do you prefer to roll your eyes and cross your arms and shake your head and tell him where to go? If you do, then I ask; do you choose a loving and passionate relationship, or do you choose a dictatorship?

*You want the best for him by actually wanting him to trust his own word first. Not yours. He can't feel safe to trust yours until he is man enough to trust his own and follow his own path.

Conclusion On Respect

When in doubt, and you're just dating a man and he is not committed; give him unconditional respect for some time. Genuine, real respect. Don't wear the pants. If after a month and you've done this genuinely, and you are not more attracted to him, and you're not 'feeling' it, then leave.
And if you're reading this and you're in a long term relationship or marriage, you do it for 90 days. Yes, 3 whole months.

Anyone who has dated knows that relationships differ a lot, and no two look the same. When it comes to giving and getting respect in your relationship, this is especially true. In some relationships, there will be a balance of respect given and received, while in others, there will be one partner who tends to hold more power. This power dynamic can also shift at different times in your relationship. And this is all normal and healthy.

Having respect in your relationship means that even though there may be disagreements from time to time, you still trust your partner, treat them with love, and have faith in their judgments. So how do you make sure the power dynamic in your relationship remains balanced more often than not?

Here are some of the best ways to give and receive respect in a relationship that may help you find the balance in yours:

Speak Up.

If you're not clear with your partner about what you want and need, then how do you expect them to know? If you don't use your voice and speak up, then you'll suffer in silence, and may grow to resent the relationship.

Nobody is a mind reader, so next time you feel like your partner is either intentionally or unintentionally being disrespectful, say something. Also if you really want to keep that power balance, encourage your partner to do the same.

Have A Life Outside The Relationship.

Feeling strong and capable outside of your relationship is important, both for you as a person and for your relationship. If the majority of one partner's happiness, identity, or fulfillment comes from the relationship, that's a lot of pressure.

In addition, that pressure can manifest itself in a lot of ways. One partner may feel suffocated, or like the relationship is becoming a burden. So in order to give respect to your partner, also give it to yourself. Your time together will be more rewarding and enjoyable if you also have time apart. I will discuss the benefits of giving your partner space in the next chapter.

Have Boundaries.

Without rules or boundaries in place, there won't be anything to draw on when it comes to talking about what's okay and what's not. Both partners should express what their own boundaries and levels of comfort are when it comes to things like flirting, finances, or family, and your partner should naturally strive to respect those.

Treat People How You Want To Be Treated.

This saying remains the Golden Rule. This saying has been repeated millions of times, but it still reigns true. Treat your partner how you would want them to treat you. If you're looking for respect, show them respect. You'll be amazed by how simple it can be.

Be Yourself.

Always stay true to who you really are, and if your partner truly loves you, they'll respect you for it. It's also a great way to show your partner that you want them to be themselves around you. Every time you show your partner more of yourself, you're inviting them to do the same. Encourage them to embrace their real selves and be more of who they already are. Then offer them a safe space to do this in it.

Stay True To Your Word.

As they say, actions speak far louder than words. If you say you're going to do something, follow through and do it.

When you follow through with something, even if it's something small like showing up at the time you said you would, you're respecting your partner and showing them you care. If you break your word, your partner won't take you as seriously, and that's when respect can be lost. So always say what you mean, and mean what you say.

Respect Yourself.

We teach others how to treat us. If you don't respect yourself first and foremost, how do you expect anyone else to? Show yourself the respect you're looking for, and you'll begin to show the people in your life how you expect to be treated.

This comes down to things like the way you talk to and about yourself, how you view yourself, and how much power you give yourself in the relationship.

Stop and think about whether you're respecting yourself enough. Because when you do, you'll encourage others to treat you the same.

Do Little Things That Show Respect.

If you want to build more respect in your relationship,

take it one step at a time. Start with small things like picking up after yourself, asking your partner about their day, or offering help without being asked.

Communicate With Respect.

When you're conversing with your partner, always be mindful about how you're speaking to them, regardless of how frustrated or upset you might be. Think about how you would like to be treated, and treat them simi-larly. Look your partner in the eye when they're talking to you, and be interested in what they have to say. Give them compliments regularly to show appreciation for who they are and what they do.

These are just a few of the small things you can do right now to give your partner more respect but they can go a long way towards creating a healthy balance in your relationship. Try them out. You may be surprised at what you find.

CHAPTER VIII

HOW TO NOT GET PLAYED IN A LONG DISTANCE RELATIONSHIP

Below is a factual story that outlines everything you need to know about a long distance relationship. True and Tested. Enjoy!

I met my partner in the oddest times when I had told myself that I'm never ever dating again. This was because I had messed up so many of my good relationships that I felt like I needed introspection. But did I really introspect?

To some extent yes! Because my last break up was the most painful of all I've ever had. If you've ever messed up a good relationship even after you were given a second chance you probably understand. The lesson I learned and understood was that one does not necessarily need a long break after a break up in order to reflect on the mistakes previously committed. The breakup process itself can be hard enough to teach you a thing or two, irrespective of how long it lasts.

Now back to the topic. Two months after the breakup I decided I was ready to mingle and I did, so everything was fine. That's when I met my partner. For someone who had committed so many mistakes I was almost certain that karma was waiting on me somewhere close ready to knock me into the grave. But haven't I endured enough really? Well, that's a story for another book. Therefore, I decided I was going to be open and clear about my intentions for once and I did.

I told her that I was at my lowest point and that I just came out of a relationship. Luckily, she needed a distraction too! Can't tell you from what though. God does work in mysterious ways indeed! That woman became everything that I needed at that time and more, the compassion and constant conversations and slowly I was starting to get up on my feet.

We became the best companions for each other from May up until November when we decided to take our relationship to the next level. If you're already thinking it yes! We fell in love. Or maybe we always were in love, just in denial.

Anyway, it gets even more interesting because the following year she was supposed to go to university in South Africa. That's when I figured our relationship wasn't going to work out and I decided to discuss it with her that I'm not a long distance relationship person. She managed to convince me otherwise however and we decided to give it a shot. After all, I didn't want to date anyone at that time so... WTF! Before she left for school, I laid down my expectations.

Your partner could be away for a job or their home is far etc and also, it's worthy to take note that the following points apply to a natural relationship where everything is relaxed and isn't forced, so your situation could be slightly different. Either way, advice is advice so my expectations were as follows:

✓ Never disappear for too long without ex plaining before or after, I prefer the former.

✓ Call every day and video call at least twice in a week.

✓ Communicate your concerns and never sleep on an unresolved issue.

✓ Have fun

These principles would seem easy at first glance until you actually have to put them into practice. Above all, they became the basic tenets of my long distance relationship and it worked out just fine for both of us. I became the happiest man alive able to work and do my activities worry-free.

Now here is where it gets tough.

My friends would explain to me that the odds for my girlfriend cheating on me while at school were very high and that she's likely to break up with me upon graduation. All that crap that makes you paranoid and doubt your relationship but I guess there was something they didn't know, the power of my four principles.

Never Disappear For Too Long Without An Explanation

According to me, this is the most important rule in a long distance relationship. You need to engage each other so much that it certainly feels like you're not distant anymore. Be it classes, lunch, shopping, school activities, visiting a friend or going out on a Friday night. You explain this to your partner because failure to do so will put ideas in your partner's head, ideas that can lead to paranoia, a fight and consequently a break up.

Imagine being in a long distance relationship and it's Friday you're having a movie night with friends. Your boyfriend hasn't checked in since 3p.m, his phone is off and it's now 11p.m.
Don't get me wrong, I'm not saying there's anything wrong with that, I'm just saying if you didn't tell your partner that you'd disappear for that long, what do you expect them to think you're doing all that time with your phone switched off? School work? Let alone the fact that everyone is out there trying their level best to convince your partner that "She's cheating on you bro, where do you think she gets sexy time from?"

The pressures that come along with being in a long distance relationship are too much to bear, they must be minimised at all costs and that is by engaging each other. You can disappear all day to visit your side guy/

girl, to go on a road trip or even a night out. All it takes is for you to make your partner aware that you intend to disappear; you won't even have to explain yourself much about where you are going if the relationship is healthy enough.

Lastly, if you were not able to inform your partner that you will disappear and are now worried about the re-action, always explain yourself before you are asked, it shows that you care and understand that they were worried about you.

The first thing you should do when you get a chance to charge your phone if your battery died, or if you forgot your phone at home is to explain and apologise. Call if you can, before attempting a text. As I said, it makes your partner see that you were worried and constantly thinking about them throughout, which is good.

If Circumstances Allow, Call Every Day And Video Call At Least Twice A Week

The secret here is to try and bring your partner as close to you as possible even in the trying times. Do you ever wonder why we usually communicate much easier on calls other than texting? That is because calls have in them the power to bring a person closer during dia-logue.

Tone and pitch are important elements of a conversa-tion and we cannot express them successfully in a text. You cannot misinterpret someone you're talking to on a call but you can misinterpret a text message. As such, calling your partner every day almost feels like actual face-to-face conversations with them, let alone when you actually see them on a video call. That way you can even get all kinky, get to flirt, etc.

You ought to be truly in love with your long distance partner in order for this to work because constant calls and texts can be annoying and boring when you run out of things to talk about. Although that is less likely to happen when you're dating your best friend, you never run out of conversations and you enjoy talking to each other.

I still remember this other time I was on call with my partner on the way from work. I decided grab some late to go lunch at some fast foods restaurant. While I was still waiting on a queue, some girl from behind attempted to make her order before me citing that I seemed busy on the phone, while on the call, I told my girlfriend that I was actually fighting for a line in a restaurant. (I let her order anyway). She then helped me put my to go food in a plastic when she realised I was struggling, with my other hand on a phone. I smiled and said thank you.

Communicate Your Concerns

Another important principle is to talk to your partner about issues that bother you and those that you think may affect your relationship. We often make the mistake of thinking that raising your concerns in a relationship is being needy or too much and that's a wrong conviction. It took me long enough to realise that for all the times that I said "It's okay!" to avoid an argument in my long distance relationship, it was actually not.

In as much as I would try to supress my feelings like that I would always burst out eventually and begin the argument all over again, this time expressing more emotion than before.

And I hate to tell you that the manner of communication from the time I avoided the argument to the time I actually voice it out is never a great one. This is where we even say the things we don't even mean because we bottle our anger until there is so much of it that it becomes difficult to put it under control when it comes out.

Never Go To Bed While There's An Unresolved Issue

It may seem pretty okay to decide to go to bed or decide to cut communication and sleep when fighting with your partner but that's never a good option. Every fight that you and your partner have has the potential to destroy or build your relationship depending on how you resolve it. Going to bed angry with unresolved issues will subconsciously push you further apart from your partner.

It is very important to talk about issues and reach a resolution on time. You don't want to give your partner a chance to weigh out her available options; to reply to that classmate or colleague who is constantly asking her to visit for movies, to start considering that lunch she's been asked to or to respond to that handsome guy she's been ignoring in her DM.

However, always try to give your partner a minimal space when needed especially after a big fight in order for both of you to reflect on the main causes of your fight but remember, it should never wait until the next day!

Have Fun

This is the most important of them all. Allowing your partner to be herself, especially at a tertiary institution where you will not always be present requires a certain level of growth. This prevents them from constantly lying to you about their activities and gives them a sense of freedom. We have seen how caged teenagers turn out when they first experience freedom in the real world, how married people often behave at tertiary institutions in the absence of their spouses.

To tell someone to not experience tertiary lifestyle at his or her prime is pretty much selfish and it usually backfires. First, we have to understand that university is fun and anything goes, so if your partner respects you and values your relationship, she will not do anything that may put your relationship in test.

Nevertheless, we cannot make the mistake of thinking they will not at any time engage in casual sexy time, have wild parties, fall for someone else or basically

dump you. That's just the way it is, people find themselves in life, they explore, they learn new things and
they move on. But love is about holding on in hope
without even forcing it.

CHAPTER IX

LET THE RELATIONSHIP BREATH
OR THEY LEAVE

The Power Of Giving Your Partner Space

Everybody needs time to themselves and I cannot stress enough how important this is for the relationship. Loving deeply doesn't mean wanting to be together every minute. When we're young and in puppy love we think maybe we could give our partners time 24/7, but that uber-romantic notion rarely sees the light of the day.

That is because we're soon sobered up to the fact that even if love may conquer all, it can't consume all. As a people we have many other things to do, some of which at times become a higher priority than spending time together, and especially when time together isn't going well.

Time together is certainly one gauge of how strong the love is. If your partner avoids intimacy all the time, there's probably a very good chance that there is a systemic incompatibility. Still, it's dangerous to put too much stock in time together as the indicator of relationship health.

An obligation to prove commitment with time can become oppressive, leading one or both partners to feel corralled, suffocated by the obligation to show up dutifully not for the fun of it but just to keep the other feeling secure.

It is important to minimize visits and sleepovers even though sometimes we overdo them unaware, and by the time it only dawns on us it's already too late. You're supposed to be able to miss your partner at least once a week and if you don't, you're probably doing something wrong.

There are certain things we're supposed to learn about ourselves as a people. Like how unhappy we get when we're broke and can't make ends meet. Now imagine if your partner was also broke and all sad at that period and you were spending some time together. The odds are that you're going to fight even over very small issues and you're not going to realize that you're only fighting because both of you are financially frustrated. The opportunity here is that you'll be discovering certain behaviours about each other and learning to resolve your issues amicably without escalating the fight. The question is, how far are you willing to go with your partner? Those small fights can easily reveal your compatibility and help you make the right choices for the future of your relationship.

Take an example of our parents who used to work in the mines in South Africa for example. They would marry their wives and then leave them at home raising kids while they go for work. Everything would turn out smoothly as they would only come back home to give their wives money or to take short leaves.

However, as soon as they get retrenched leaving them no choice but to go spend the rest of their lives with their wives together, things start to get sour at home. I took my time to investigate and think about why this happens and this is the conclusion I came to:

- **Monied men make no mistakes**
- **Unemployed men are very insecure**

Monied Men Make No Mistakes

We need to understand that in the eyes of the people around us, we're usually only as good as the size of our wallets. Therefore, if you think rich people get away with things easily, it's not just them, it's everyone who has the means. Take some time to think about that family relative whom everyone listens to at family gatherings and funerals - his word is the last and nothing carries on in his absence.

That is the power of being able to provide and so is the case in relationships. When you hold the means of income, you're automatically exempted from dating headaches. Remember that women always put it out there that it's better for them to be cheated on by a rich man than a broke man because if they're dating the former, they'd simply drive themselves to the nearest spar and have their problems massaged away. This clearly tells us that as a man, you have only one job, and the job is to make money.

The Most Sensitive A Man Can Be Is When He Has No Job

Secondly, I learned that the lowest point a man can be is when he is broke. This comes from the notion that men are by right wired to be providers and if they cannot provide, they eventually don't feel like they're men enough. They become very sensitive to anything, especially comments their friends and partners make.

This is the time when they need respect and support the most. You would confront him about seemingly minor things like food and he will silently attribute it to the fact that you're probably confronting him because he is out of work. While that happens, some men develop a defence mechanism by becoming very violent or abusive, while some just decide to observe and endure in silence.

In becoming abusive, it gives them a sense of power that they are still in control, while in actuality it only drives their partners away. It always seems as if most women leave their partners whey they become broke and out of work but the reality may be that their partners have become impossible to stay with.

The truth is that women are not wired to become providers, having to take care of their partners overwhelms them. They mainly lose respect and support for their partners because of unemployment, some men take it all in for a moment but as soon as they find themselves financially, they will leave the relationship.

So in a nutshell, if you intend to keep your partner through thick and thin, be weary of how you address issues with him, support him and most importantly respect him like never before. All this can be done while you're encouraging him to get another job, buying him newspapers to check for vacancies and supporting him in all you can without hurting his ego.

CHAPTER X

THE NOTION OF A SIDE-CHICK

Hooking-up seems all fun and frolic until one of you catches feelings. Alternatively, we can say that's how every romantic movie starts. However, can real life really lead on from reel life? Times have changed and so have people's opinion on the matters of love.

What you really think is love, in reality, might just be lust and things come to an ugly turn when only one partner in a relationship is hit by this. Before hitting the apparent stronger sex with the ultimate chick question, "Who we are?" Ask yourself! Are you really his girlfriend or just his menial hook-up side-chick that he just happened to treat with respect?

It has been rightly said that it is a tough task to read a woman's mind indeed. In today's fast pacing world, everybody is busily engaged in his or her own problems. Nobody wants this extra responsibility of having to deal with a relationship too. So what came next? The trend of open relationships and casual relationships strictly pertaining to being sexual in nature rarely garnished with a pinch of friendship.

As a result, slangs like 'f**kboy' and 'side-chick' came into existence.

However, the real questions are, are you a side-chick for real? Are you commitment phobic and only have a good time when in casual relationships?

Some side-chicks can be sadists too. Ladies that tend to go after a man who is already in a relationship or married often end up creating a ruckus for all the people involved, mostly on purpose. Nevertheless, sometimes the former doesn't feel like hurting anybody else's feelings, but still, want to engage in a fun-filled ride.

Here's How To Know If You Might Be A Potential Side-Chick Or Not!

What are the qualities of a side-chick, you'd ask? However, a side-chick isn't always born (just sometimes...) and there are times when you happen to turn into a side-chick.

This might be due to some bad past experience in a relationship or due to the media hype. Most of the times, they are a nuisance to the society and if you identify a promiscuous creature like this in your life, steer clear!

Side-chicks fall under the ultimate sadist category and only believe in feeding their own ego and selfish needs. Their most common weapon being sexy time, they tend to make the first move and seduce the guy, so as to engage in an activity that he might regret in the future.

If you can relate to this information and are a lady, you will perhaps know what I am saying. But is this something that you should be proud of? Obviously, not! The aftermath doesn't bother, and you simply don't care about other people's feelings. It's not the fact that they are dead inside, but the fact that they attain some kind of selfish pleasure in making other people's lives a mess, playing with their feelings and not caring by the end of it all!

A side-chick is just a female version of a 'f**kboy' to categorise it in the simplest of words.

There might also be a possibility that you are treated or forced to act as a side-chick due to the situation or just involuntarily without even knowing it. When a guy is already into a relationship or married and engages in any kind of sexual or emotional activity with another woman, that 'other' woman is the 'side-chick'.

Just like a little devil, they will make efforts to know about a man's personal life and dwell on it to create strategies as to how to ruin it in order to feed their own selfish needs.

Some women tend to chase committed men just to challenge themselves or to see if they can actually grab something out of reach. Sometimes to establish if karma had already closed its doors. They take it as a challenge and chase it until it's achieved or until they wreck their lives.

She is a little predator that is very dangerous and all must be cautious of and avoid her at all costs. Do not fall for that pretty face, all you committed boys!

They are not just famous for wreaking havoc in people's lives, but there are reasons as to why they do it. For one, they're like the silent private creatures of the night and loyalty means nothing to them. They may even blackmail you after all is done and said for money! And yes, I've read and seen cases. This act is commonly more than being true.

A side-chick is just a bummed out word for what the previous generation used to call a 'mistress'. She engages in sexual activity with more than one sexual partner at the same period of time, strictly avoiding any kind of emotional feelings.

But most often, the side-chick is unaware of her position. She might be treated as a side-chick by the guy without her prior knowledge into the relationship. The next time you date someone, try to figure out or better, make sure the guy is single as a pringle or if he is just admitting to being one. Because if he lies, even before you know it, you are his side-chick, his backup or the other woman in his life.

Some men just don't believe in the theory of monogamy, and same goes for the ladies as well. Therefore, what follows next is the creation of a batter of a nuisance that affects all of us!

To be frank with you, the fact that you're asking yourself if you're a side chick may be because you are. That's why it's important to know all the signs that will help you know if you may be one. Below is a list of some useful questions to ask yourself in determining if you may be a side chick or not:

- Can you call him at any time of the day and does he answer or does he keep conversations short and always miss your calls due to whatever reasons or excuses he makes?

- How often do you see this person and when you do, how long do you spend time together? Is it during the day when he should be in school or working or does he stay the night?

- Does he hide his phone or ignore calls while he is with you or is his phone always on silent mode?

- How well do you know him, his family or friends etc.? Do you have knowledge of his history with past relationships?

- What's making you wonder if you are a side chick?

Side-chicks are not heartless or dead inside. They will take out time and make efforts for you to fall into their pit. Just because they go out for lunch and drinks with you doesn't necessarily mean she might be going out just with you.

She will message you every other day knowing you already have a girlfriend and lets you engage in conversations that she knows you might not want to avoid.

Maybe it's a football match or maybe it's just sexual, but they are trick monsters, often possessing experience in the matter!

If she tells you she likes you but you still think that she does not have all the ears for you when you talk to her or that she doesn't remember any important event that might be precious to you, maybe she is not the serious kind and just craves for the warmth of affection that you tend to gain in a relationship.

People date because they like each other and have genuine feelings for each other but what if she fakes it just to make you believe that she loves you? This might be a secret but nothing like something that doesn't exist. Maybe she has told this to a couple of guys and fails to show you her phone in the name of trust.

Some other important factors to take note of might be if you have met her on social media or some social dating site, then there might be a high chance that she is smart enough to know that it's the best option for engaging in promiscuity and she uses it to the fullest to fulfill this purpose.

If you really like this girl and still have doubts about her loyalty, make sure you dig into the minute details like how much time she spends on her phone or the fact that she has just recently ended or came out of a relationship. She might even use you as a scapegoat for a rebound.

Sometimes girls already know the status of a guy and are okay with it or will be okay with being the other half. I'm not saying that they lack in self-respect (or maybe a little) but attempting to wreak havoc in somebody else's relationship or for their own selfish needs, a side-chick is not always unaware of her status and she is always happy to see other's in pain. But for women with self-respect and who happen to find themselves in a situation relating to a similar ideology of thought and lots of doubt, here comes the newsflash!

How Not To Be A Side-Chick Anymore

Respect Yourself

Ladies, before anything else, respect yourself and keep in mind the fact that there are many boys out there and life won't end for you if you cannot achieve the one who is already committed. Put your energies into making yourself better for your own self and not for anybody else!

Understand That This Is Not A Game

Most women tend to have a habit to show other women down. So they do not complain against the attention they receive from somebody else's boyfriend. This is a very common habit that people tend to mistake for a game which is not cool. If you have any past grudges against a person regarding some past issue, talk to them instead of taking revenge on them by stealing their boyfriend.

You Don't Have To Prove Your Worth

There are ladies and men alike that tend to commit this kind of revenge on someone that they might have a grudge against either currently or previously. I have heard people confess that they only cheated on their enemy's boyfriend to hurt their feelings and win. Understand that this is not a game and you don't have to win it in order to prove your worth. Understand that your previous friendships and jealousy are different and attempting to interfere in somebody's personal life is different.

Realise That This Can Only Do Harm

You have to realize this one important fact that engaging in an act of playing with someone's life will only lead you to a dead end besides harming some people's feelings that you unintentionally or intentionally intended to do. Spilling dirt on others will only get you dirty, instead, put all this energy to good use in bettering yourself! Unless of course you have signed a better deal with karma.

Get Into A Serious Relationship

And be loyal to too! One of the best things that you can do to get your mind off engaging in playful games for fun is to get yourself a man that is true and loyal to you and treat him the same. Focus on yourself and your new budding relationship and think of things to spice up your relationship instead of souring others.

Drop The Jealousy

If you do not want to admit it but understand that you are in some way jealous of the other girl and want to seek her attention by approaching her boyfriend, then drop this attitude and make your life worthwhile by doing something good for the others or yourself. If you have anger against a person, then put your anger and energy to a good productive use. You can join a gym or take up meditation to calm and distract yourself.

Can A Side Chick Turn Into A Main Chick?

Yes! But the chances are very slim. You've got to be really lucky to be able to lure a guy into leaving his girlfriend for you.

If you intend on delving into this adventure, here are a few things you need to know. Avoid ill-speaking his girlfriend. Side chicks who make silly comments about the Main are more likely to be heartbroken than not. That is because they unknowingly compel the guy to want to protect the image of the Main. This they do by breaking your heart so that you may know you're not better than the main chick because she was chosen over you.

Some other factor to consider is that cheating is morally wrong. You cannot build your relationship on the tears of the other girl and expect things to go smoothly for you. I understand that at times these people may be our soul mates in the wrong hands but is it really worth risking your health and time for?

If you are dealing with a similar situation, you must talk it out with someone and get it out of your system. You can either talk to a friend, the guy or even a therapist for that matter, i.e., if you fail to feel any kind of empathy even if you want to, you might be suffering from Empathy Deficit Disorder which can be treated with regular therapy.

Else, if you happen to find yourself in such a situation and recognize your position as a side-chick, you can back off for good. Backing off will prevent a lot of problems for all the people involved.

There might also be a chance that you happen to find yourself in such a position without knowing anything about the situation, in that case, you can clear your doubts and talk to a friend or the guy himself. Confront him about the situation and ask him what he really wants or whom he really desires and wants to be with. If it's not you, walk away and never look back.

The Type Of Men You Should Avoid

Fake relationships are the types I should define as ones without satisfaction. If you are in a relationship and you are not enjoying your partner then it should be defined as fake relationships. In most cases, ladies are at the receiving end of fake relationships.

However, you might be attracted by the charming

words and sweet gestures of a man. And you will become ecstatic that your prince charm is finally here. Of course, some guys make it "as long and happy as possible" for you, but those mentioned in this message are not. So, please stay away from this type of men.

We know that the perfect man does not exist. Yes, not the perfect girl too! Of course, each person will have some negative features, but there must be a limit, right? There are some types of men who cannot bear any woman. You may be hopelessly in love with them. Therefore, you need open your eyes, or at least your brain. It's good to be a bit blind in love, but do not be stupid because it might lead to an abusive relationship if not fake relationships.

So here are some types of guys you should not stay long with. Kindly check if the man you are dating fits into one of these types because it's time to say good-bye. However, for the guys who read this, if you think you belong to one of the following, try to improve your ways.

The Mama's Boy

Let me first mention this; I do not mean that someone who loves his mother and cares for his mother is terrible. In fact, it's a big turn. However, there must be a rule, a limit. Every little thing cannot be done except according to his mother. Imagine that the man asks his mother what to wear or what to eat, or to continually talk to the phone when he is with you. Not cool.

The Rebound Guy

This guy is not older than his ex, and you're just a distraction for him. Ouch! That hurts, but it's true! He just needs someone to forget about his beloved ex. He will keep comparing your little things with her. Talking about your ex is okay but obsessive about her, probably not.

The Man Child

The man-child or the peter-pan just does not want to grow. He only lives from his parents' money or just works to pay off his bills. Also, he continually needs you to take care of him. He behaves like a high school child and demands that you cook for him and feed him. Dating him is the same as adopting an overweight child. Hopefully, you do not want to do that.

The One Who Never is Around

You have to wait for his answer for hours; He will never pick your call and will call you back whenever he wants to. You do not have to be with someone that you consider to be selfish. Forget to feel special and loved; He's not even there if you need him most. He will call you when he wants you. He will make plans without talking to you. Why do you need this guy, just dump him!

The Liar

This type of guy is a compulsive liar. Also, he will lie about his relationships, career, salary, home or car. He just wants to sketch a rosy image of his perfect life to impress you. Once you fall for him, little moment to enjoy with him, and you will realise that he is not the man for which you fell, even not close. Whatever the reason is, lying is not cool. The fact is that you don't deserve such guy.

The guy who never pays

He asked you out and asked you to pay because he doesn't have money. Okay, you paid, but what if this happens regularly? Girl, it's time to dump this loser, who will not even share the bill with you. We do not expect the man to pay for all dates, but he can offer or split the account at any rate. This one just wants to have his cake and eat.

The Obsessed One

He is obsessed with you. He wants to talk to you every day. If you do not meet him, he will appear at your workplace, school or home; He will ask you every move, he wants to know everything about you. The man does not know how to give space or respect your personal life.
Sharing is good, but if he starts telling you where to go and where not, that's too much. He wants you alone, all for himself. No doubt, this is an evident obsession which is not cute at all. So take him away before he becomes a burden for you.

The Needy One

Even the thought of this guy is enough to make me angry. He is very excited and will love you like a parasite. He will always send you texts, wants to meet you every day, always wants to talk to you. I'm sure you do not have so much patience. Just get rid of him because you are in a fake relationship.

The Cheater

He has played falsely in the past and will be fake in the future. There is nothing bad giving room for a second chance to someone you love, but there's some regret to be shown by the man. If he just tries to find excuses and is not ready to accept his mistakes, then it does not make sense to be with him. He is interested in every woman he is watching. Even when he is with you, he will look shamelessly on other women. You do not need such a mess or fake relationships, just let him go.

The flirting Type

He is handsome and oh so charming. He knows how to make you fall for him. Yes, behind all those flirtatious texts he's dating many girls and then choosing the best options thereafter. You can never expect to be a priority with this man.

If he is free on Friday night, he will call you. However, if he has better options, he will come up with some apologies. It is difficult for girls to resist those sweeter-than-honey words and sparkling eyes. He's just going to play with you until he's bored. So you're just wasting your time.

The Commitment Phobia

This type of man is found abundantly. He likes to go out

with you, he loves to have a walk with you, but he will not commit to you. He will have a story about how a girl broke his heart or bring some boring stories. Whatever the reason, do not go out with him unless you're just looking for a flirt. Everything will look perfect, but you can never get security and love from him.

The Narcissistic Type

He is probably handsome, but, according to him, he is the most good-looking man in the world. He will take more time to be ready than you. Also, he will use an abundance of beauty products to maintain his turbulent appearance, and he will never criticise his appearance in a negative way.

CHAPTER I

THE PSYCHOLOGY OF PLAYERS

A Brief Overview

Before delving into the psyche of players it's important to first delve into the psyche of the girls they target or who fall victim to their charms.

The girls who fall for the trap of these players are usually no simple, regular, ordinary girls and although not all the time, girls with low self-esteem… they are usually the girls who want only the best things in life; it can either be items of luxury or good-looking boyfriends. It is a common notion that some girls ordinarily take their validation from rubbing shoulders with good looking famous guys, it probably makes them feel better about themselves we don't know.

Guys who can impress their inner circle and make other girls jealous or envious of themselves are usually the vital component of this phenomenon. In fact, put in simpler words, players hardly ever sleep with women who envy them, that way they'd be breaking the most vital rule which is to "Never sleep with your crushes; it is because of them that all the girls want you."

To players, these are the women who tell every girl how good they smell, how expensive their wardrobe is or how phat their wallet is. So why would players ruin their only means for attracting more women to increase their body count over a shameless orgasm? If anything, players would rather impress their female admirers by giving them cash and occasionally buying them gifts with the hope that they may tell all their female friends about it.

So not every guy who is good to you is actually good, he might just be using you to communicate to your friends. They usually prefer the extrovert girls with many friends to which they can easily make their pick.

Understand that by being good-looking, smart and socially popular players realize their value proposition, which is basically what they offer to the other gender, their market price as well as how much demand-supply mismatch favours them in the mating game. We cannot hide from the reality that no girl wants to date a typical guy whom nobody knows, let alone if he has no outstanding talent or a known record of women he had dated in the past, or the available record is as uncertain as a rap career in Lesotho.

It is worthy to note that unfortunately, this is why players lie a lot in the dating game, they try so hard to fill the position of an ideal boyfriend that they find themselves having to use anything that will put them in that position. You find out after giving it all up that the penthouse he took you to belongs to his friend while the BMW Motorsport that got you taking selfies and live videos is his dad's (who is probably out on a business trip to china)

Depending on how high the girls have set their market price, players will do anything and everything to beat that price, even if it means lying about his age, his career, his wealth, his home or his interest, as long as it will land him right into your pants.
It's easier for them to lie because they don't intend on hanging around you for too long and this happens a lot at parties or night clubs. This way they can easily blame the alcohol when confronted about the lies.

Although this is the hard pill to swallow, girls should understand that the person they're looking for is usually the low key guy who seems a little insecure by a mere look of an eye until you have the first date with him, perhaps second as well. I will explain why going on a date is important before entering into a relationship and why we should embrace the culture later in the book.

ABOUT THE AUTHOR

Mohosho Pofane

I don't really like to talk about myself because I don't
want it to look like I'm bragging or
anything, you see? 
Those "I have a degree in 1 and 2 and I
have achieved
3 and 4. Who cares about any of that?
This is a book
about relationships and dating! They don't teach you
that in school do they?

THE END